MY DAD'S FULL NAME: _____

DATE OF BIRTH: _____

PLACE OF BIRTH: _____

MY DAD'S MOTHER'S FULL NAME: _____

DATE OF BIRTH: _____

PLACE OF BIRTH: _____

MY DAD'S FATHER'S FULL NAME: _____

DATE OF BIRTH: _____

PLACE OF BIRTH: _____

DAD, YOUR LIFE IS A GIFT.

YOU HOLD WITHIN YOU A STORY THAT ONLY YOU
CAN SHARE. USE THESE PAGES TO FILL WITH YOUR
ONE-OF-A-KIND MEMORIES—WHETHER IT'S A SPECIAL
MOMENT FROM YOUR CHILDHOOD, AN UNFORGETTABLE
ADVENTURE, OR A PIECE OF ADVICE TO PASS ON.

SPEAK FROM THE HEART, IN YOUR OWN WORDS—IT
DOESN'T NEED TO BE FORMAL OR COMPLEX. BECAUSE
WHEN YOU ARE FINISHED, YOU WILL CREATE A GIFT
THAT WILL BE LOVED FOR GENERATIONS.

CHILDHOOD HOME

WHAT WAS YOUR HOME LIKE GROWING UP? INCLUDE DETAILS ABOU
THE NEIGHBORHOOD, WHO LIVED WITH YOU, WHAT YOUR ROOM WA
LIKE, AND HOW AND WHERE YOUR FAMILY SPENT TIME TOGETHER.

WE DO NOT REMEMBER DAYS,
WE REMEMBER MOMENTS.

—CESARE PAVESE—

HOLIDAY TRADITIONS

YOUR FAVORITE HOLIDAY GROWING UP WAS:

SOME FAMILY HOLIDAY TRADITIONS WERE:

MEMORABLE GIFTS (BIG OR SMALL)
YOU RECEIVED WERE:

FAMILY RELATIONSHIPS

WHAT WAS YOUR RELATIONSHIP WITH YOUR PARENTS LIKE?
DID YOU HAVE SPECIAL RELATIONSHIPS WITH ANY OTHER
FAMILY MEMBERS?

NAMES

_____

NICKNAMES YOU'VE HAD:

WHERE THEY CAME FROM:

NAMES OF PETS YOU'VE HAD:

NAMES OF CHILDHOOD FRIENDS:

WHAT WERE YOUR FRIENDS LIKE?

BEING A KID

WHAT DO YOU MISS MOST ABOUT BEING A KID? IT COULD
BE A SPECIFIC ACTIVITY OR PERHAPS A FEELING YOU MISS.

...CHILDHOOD
LASTS ALL
THROUGH LIFE.

—GASTON BACHELARD—

FIRST MEMORIES

MY EARLIEST MEMORY IS:

WHEN I WAS LITTLE, I WOULD GET TO SCHOOL BY:

AS A CHILD, I WAS AFRAID OF:

MY FAVORITE TOYS WERE:

I'VE ALWAYS HAD A NATURAL TALENT FOR:

SOME OF THE CHORES I HAD GROWING UP WERE:

MY FIRST PAYING JOB WAS:

I WAS PAID THIS MUCH:

A truly rich man

IS ONE WHOSE CHILDREN

run into his arms

WHEN HIS HANDS ARE EMPTY.

—UNKNOWN—

GETTING INTO MISCHIEF

WHAT ARE ONE OR TWO THINGS YOU DID THAT YOU NEVER
TOLD YOUR PARENTS ABOUT? WHAT RULES DID YOUR PARENTS
HAVE, AND WHICH ONES DID YOU TEST THE MOST?

SCHOOL DAYS

NAMES OF SCHOOLS YOU ATTENDED:

YOUR FAVORITE SUBJECTS IN SCHOOL:

DO YOU REMEMBER ANY FAVORITE TEACHERS? WHAT WERE THEIR NAMES, AND WHY WERE THEY SPECIAL?

WHAT DID YOU WANT TO BE WHEN YOU GREW UP?
(AND IT COULD BE MULTIPLE THINGS.)

GOING PLACES

WHERE ARE SOME INTERESTING PLACES YOU'VE VISITED?
WHAT MADE THEM SO MEMORABLE?

_____

_____

_____

_____

_____

_____

_____

_____

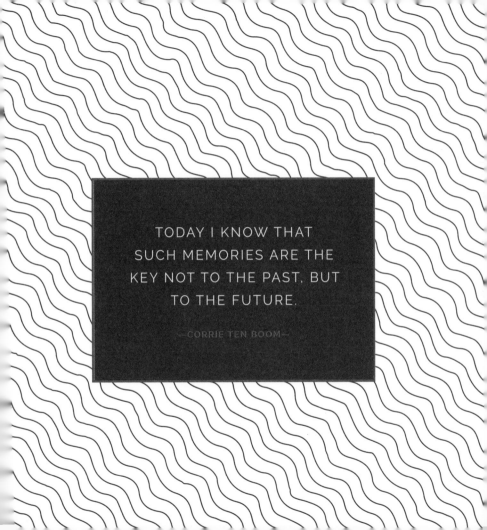

TODAY I KNOW THAT
SUCH MEMORIES ARE THE
KEY NOT TO THE PAST, BUT
TO THE FUTURE.

—CORRIE TEN BOOM—

FREE TIME

FAVORITE CHILDHOOD BOOKS:

FAVORITE CHILDHOOD TV SHOWS:

FAVORITE CHILDHOOD MUSIC:

FAVORITE CHILDHOOD GAMES OR SPORTS:

FAVORITE CHILDHOOD HOBBIES, INTERESTS,
OR COLLECTIONS:

TIME TRAVEL

IF YOU COULD GO BACK IN TIME TO RELIVE ANY MOMENT
IN YOUR LIFE, WHAT WOULD IT BE AND WHY?

_____

_____

_____

_____

_____

_____

_____

...HISTORY ISN'T JUST
THE PAST. IT'S ALIVE IN US.

—NATALIE PORTMAN—

DEFINING SUCCESS

WHAT DOES SUCCESS MEAN TO YOU?

WHO ARE SOME PEOPLE YOU BELIEVE ARE SUCCESSFUL?

HOW HAVE YOU BEEN SUCCESSFUL?

...HIS HERITAGE TO HIS
CHILDREN WASN'T WORDS,
OR POSSESSIONS, BUT AN

UNSPOKEN TREASURE, THE
TREASURE OF HIS EXAMPLE
AS A *man* AND A *father*.

—WILL ROGERS JR.—

BEING A FATHER

WHAT WAS IT LIKE TO BECOME A FATHER? WHAT ARE
SOME OF YOUR VERY FIRST MEMORIES OF YOUR CHILDREN?

FAMILY TRAITS

WAYS YOUR CHILDREN ARE LIKE YOU
OR THEIR OTHER PARENT:

MEMORY MAKING

WHAT ARE SOME OF YOUR FAVORITE THINGS YOU'VE
DONE WITH YOUR CHILDREN?

THE MOST
PRECIOUS THING
A PARENT CAN GIVE A CHILD
IS A LIFETIME OF HAPPY
MEMORIES.

—FRANK TYGER—

MOMENTS OF LAUGHTER

LIST 5 MEMORIES OF WHEN YOUR CHILDREN WERE
YOUNG THAT STILL MAKE YOU LAUGH:

SIGNS OF AFFECTION

HOW DO YOU SHOW YOUR LOVE TO YOUR CHILDREN? DO YOU SHOWER
THEM WITH GIFTS? PRAISE THEIR SUCCESSES? MAYBE YOU GENTLY
ENCOURAGE THEM TO DO THEIR BEST OR HAVE A SPECIAL TRADITION
JUST BETWEEN YOU. SHARE YOUR THOUGHTS HERE:

_____

_____

_____

_____

_____

_____

_____

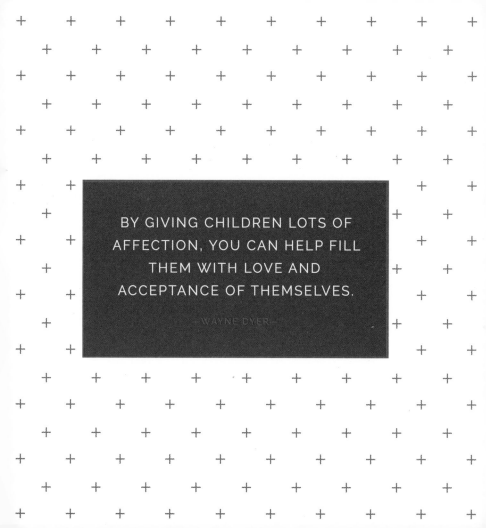

BY GIVING CHILDREN LOTS OF
AFFECTION, YOU CAN HELP FILL
THEM WITH LOVE AND
ACCEPTANCE OF THEMSELVES.

—WAYNE DYER—

WORDS TO REMEMBER

THINGS YOU'VE OFTEN SAID TO YOUR KIDS:

_____

_____

_____

_____

_____

_____

_____

THINGS YOUR CHILDREN HAVE SAID
THAT YOU'LL NEVER FORGET:

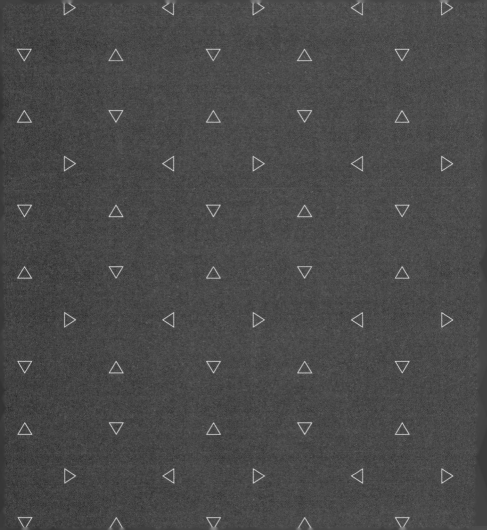

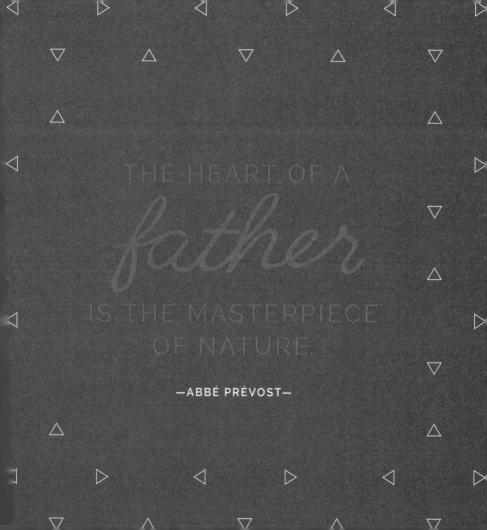

THE HEART OF A

father

IS THE MASTERPIECE
OF NATURE.

—ABBÉ PRÉVOST—

ROLE MODELS

WHO ARE SOME PEOPLE YOU ADMIRE AND WHY?
THEY COULD BE LIFELONG FRIENDS, CELEBRITIES,
FAMILY MEMBERS, ETC.

FAVORITES

ONE OF YOUR FAVORITE COLORS IS:

MOST DAYS, YOU'RE WEARING:

YOUR FAVORITE DESSERT IS:

A SMELL THAT MAKES YOU STOP EVERY TIME IS:

YOU LOVE PLAYING THIS GAME:

A BOOK THAT HAS STUCK WITH YOU IS:

MUSIC YOU LOVE TO LISTEN TO IS:

YOUR FAVORITE MOVIE OF ALL TIME IS:

YOU'RE HAPPIEST WHEN YOU ARE:

WORDS YOU TRY TO LIVE BY ARE:

FAMILY RESEMBLANCE

WHAT ARE SOME WAYS YOU ARE LIKE
YOUR PARENTS? HOW ARE YOU DIFFERENT?

_____

_____

_____

_____

_____

_____

_____

THE BEST THING TO
HOLD ONTO IN LIFE
IS EACH OTHER.

—AUDREY HEPBURN—

YOUR BEST QUALITIES

WHAT ARE SOME THINGS PEOPLE OFTEN
COMPLIMENT YOU ON?

WHICH ONE MEANS THE MOST TO YOU AND WHY?

_____

_____

_____

_____

_____

_____

_____

PERSONALITY TRAITS

WHAT ABOUT YOU HAS STAYED THE SAME THROUGHOUT
YOUR LIFE? WHAT'S CHANGED?

_____

_____

_____

_____

_____

_____

_____

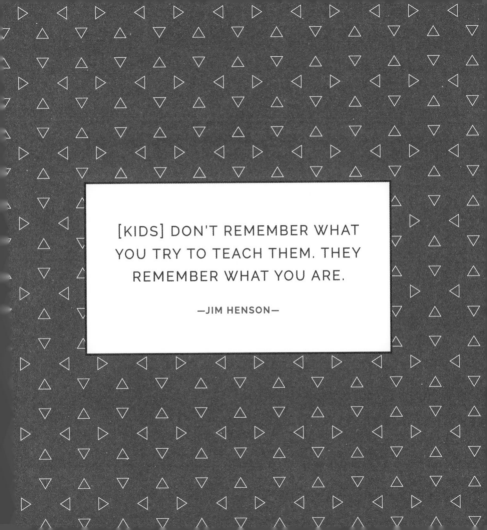

[KIDS] DON'T REMEMBER WHAT YOU TRY TO TEACH THEM. THEY REMEMBER WHAT YOU ARE.

—JIM HENSON—

LIFE MOTTO

WHAT IS YOUR FAVORITE QUOTE OR SAYING? OR MAYBE
YOU HAVE SEVERAL? SHARE THEM HERE AND DESCRIBE
WHAT THEY MEAN TO YOU.

THE LOVE WE GIVE AWAY IS

THE ONLY LOVE WE KEEP.

—ELBERT HUBBARD—

GREAT LOVES

WHO HAVE BEEN YOUR GREATEST LOVES THROUGHOUT
YOUR LIFE? WHAT DID THEY MEAN TO YOU, AND HOW HAVE
THEY CHANGED YOUR LIFE FOR THE BETTER?

THREE THINGS

---

3 THINGS YOU'RE PROUD OF:

---

3 THINGS YOU'RE PASSIONATE ABOUT:

---

3 THINGS YOU'VE LOST:

_____

_____

_____

3 THINGS YOU LOOK FORWARD TO:

_____

_____

_____

LIFE LESSONS

WHAT WAS ONE OF THE TOUGHEST LESSONS
YOU'VE LEARNED IN LIFE? HOW HAS IT CHANGED YOU
(FOR BETTER OR WORSE)?

OTHER THINGS MAY
CHANGE US, BUT WE START
AND END WITH FAMILY.

— ANTHONY BRANDT—

PLACES I'VE LIVED

LIST THE PLACES THAT YOU'VE LIVED
THROUGHOUT YOUR LIFE:

WHILE WE TRY TO TEACH
OUR CHILDREN ALL ABOUT LIFE,
OUR CHILDREN TEACH US
what life is all about.

— ANGELA SCHWINDT—

FUTURE DREAMS

WHAT WOULD YOU LIKE TO DO IN YOUR LIFETIME?

_____

_____

_____

_____

_____

_____

_____

WORLD EVENTS

SIGNIFICANT EVENTS THAT HAPPENED IN YOUR LIFE:

EVENT: _____

WHEN IT HAPPENED: _____

WHERE YOU WERE: _____

HOW IT AFFECTED YOU: _____

_____

_____

_____

_____

EVENT: _____

WHEN IT HAPPENED: _____

WHERE YOU WERE: _____

HOW IT AFFECTED YOU: _____

_____

_____

EVENT: _____

WHEN IT HAPPENED: _____

WHERE YOU WERE: _____

HOW IT AFFECTED YOU: _____

_____

_____

THE BEST OF FATHERHOOD

WHAT'S THE BIGGEST CHALLENGE ABOUT BEING A FATHER?
WHAT'S THE BEST THING ABOUT BEING A FATHER?

...THERE ARE ONLY TWO LASTING BEQUESTS WE CAN HOPE TO GIVE OUR CHILDREN. ONE OF THESE... IS ROOTS, THE OTHER, WINGS.

—HODDING CARTER—

GIVING THANKS

LIST 10 THINGS YOU'RE GRATEFUL FOR IN YOUR LIFE:

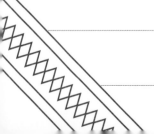

SOUND ADVICE

IF YOU COULD PASS ALONG ONE PIECE OF ADVICE,
WHAT WOULD IT BE?

A LASTING WISH

WHAT WISHES DO YOU HAVE FOR YOUR CHILDREN?

_____

_____

_____

_____

_____

_____

_____

CHILDREN WILL NOT REMEMBER
YOU FOR THE MATERIAL THINGS YOU
PROVIDED BUT FOR THE FEELING
THAT YOU CHERISHED THEM.

—RICHARD L. EVANS—

WITH SPECIAL THANKS TO THE ENTIRE COMPENDIUM FAMILY.

CREDITS:
WRITTEN BY: MIRIAM HATHAWAY
DESIGNED BY: JESSICA PHOENIX
EDITED BY: AMELIA RIEDLER

ISBN: 978-1-943200-43-6